Adventures of Noah

ISBN 978-0-578-50271-7 (hardcover)

Lorus PL
P. O. Box 490425
Leesburg, FL 34749
407-270-3660
IG AdventuresofNoah2018

Printed in the United States of America

Adventures of Noah

Lori Brown

Hello, I am Noah, and I am a puppy. Let me tell you a little about myself.

My adventure begins when I was born. I was born a blue tick hound and beagle mix. That's right. Not just one breed, but two. I know I am a different mixture.

My head looks like a beagle, and the rest of my body looks like blue tick hound. I am black, brown, and white in color. But even my color is unique.

My legs, from my knees down, are brown and white spots. And from my knees up, I am black and white. I really have some cool patterns. I am a unique but very cute puppy. At least I think so.

I was born with two other brothers. My brothers were just as cute as I am, same colors as I have, just different patterns.

None of our faces look the same.

We were all approximately two and a half months old when someone gave us to an animal shelter to save us. We were happy! We were fed, had shelter, and even had a nice bed to sleep on. We didn't know there was a better place for us to be.

13

One day, a man named Russell called to see one of my brothers. He and his wife, Lori, were shopping on the internet and fell in love with my brother Nic. They couldn't come to visit Nic because they weren't in town. They had to wait until they came back home to come see us.

In the meantime, my brothers and I would play inside and outside, and really, we thought life was okay.

One of the days that I was playing with my brothers while waiting for the couple to return home, another family came by and adopted my brother Nic before the other couple could get home to see him.

I will admit, my brother Nic was just as adorable as I am, just in his own way.

A couple more days went by, and that couple called to see if Nic was still available or there to adopt. The animal shelter told them, "No, but Nic does have two brothers that we do still have."

So Russell and Lori were still excited. They were sad that they couldn't adopt Nic but were happy to learn there were two more brothers available.

Since they were home, they rushed over to see us.

There we were, looking so handsome in our kennel. They wanted to hold me, but they weren't allowed just yet.

They looked at me, looked at my other brother, Nikee,

and then they slowly walked away.

They had to fill out an application and go through the normal process. Basically, they had to prove to the shelter they knew how to properly take care of me. To make sure we were a good fit.

A few hours went by, and they were back! They had filled out their application and did whatever the shelter asked them to do.

This time when they came back to my kennel, they were allowed to hold me.

Betty, one of the staff, opened up my kennel door, and then the couple talked with each other a little bit.

Next thing I know, I was being lifted up by the man Russell. He held me for a little while, then gave me to his wife, Lori. She held me for a little while.

A minute or two went by, and I was handed back to Betty.

Once again, they walked away.

Betty put me back in my kennel and walked away too.

A little bit of time went by, and next thing I know, Betty came back to my kennel, opened the door, and picked me up.

She walked me into a different area and gave me a bath. I was now getting a bath.

After more time went by, Betty brought me to the front of the building where the couple was.

They adopted me!

About the Author

Lori and her husband (along with Noah, of course) live in Florida.

www.ingramcontent.com/pod-product-compliance
Lightning Source LLC
Chambersburg PA
CBHW040256100426
42811CB00011B/1282